D0235745

LINKING THE PAST AND PRESENT

WHAT DID THE
VIKINGS
DO FOR ME?

Elizabeth Raum

www.raintreepublishers.co.uk
Visit our website to find out more information about Raintree books.

To order:

☎ Phone 0845 6044371

🖶 Fax +44 (0) 1865 312263

🖳 Email myorders@raintreepublishers.co.uk

Customers from outside the UK please telephone +44 1865 312262

Raintree is an imprint of Capstone Global Library Limited, a company incorporated in England and Wales having its registered office at 7 Pilgrim Street, London, EC4V 6LB - Registered company number: 6695582

Edited by Megan Cotugno and Laura Knowles
Designed by Richard Parker
Original illustrations © Capstone Global Library Limited 2010
Illustrated by Roger@KJA-artists.com
Picture research by Hannah Taylor
Originated by Capstone Global Library Limited
Printed and bound in China by CTPS

ISBN 978 0 431082 59 2 (hardback)
14 13 12 11 10
10 9 8 7 6 5 4 3 2 1

British Library Cataloguing in Publication Data
Raum, Elizabeth.
What did the Vikings do for me?. -- (Linking the past and present)
948'.022-dc22
A full catalogue record for this book is available from the British Library.

Acknowledgements

We would like to thank the following for permission to reproduce photographs: Alamy Images p. **8** (© OJPHOTOS); The Bridgeman Art Library pp. **7** (© Nationalmuseum, Stockholm, Sweden), **21** (Private Collection); Corbis pp. **11** (Image Source), **17** (Ted Spiegel); Getty Images pp. **10** (The Bridgeman Art Library/ William Gersham Collingwood), **18** (Hulton Archive), **23** (National Geographic/ Peter V. Bianchi), **26** (AFP Photo/ Carl De Souza), **27** (AFP Photo/ Patrik Stollarz); shutterstock p. **13** (© Sally Wallis); Topfoto p. **9**.

Cover photograph of Gaia, replica Viking ship, Norway reproduced with permission of Photolibrary/Robert Harding Travel Library.

We would like to thank Dr Chris Callow for his invaluable help in the preparation of this book.

Every effort has been made to contact copyright holders of material reproduced in this book. Any omissions will be rectified in subsequent printings if notice is given to the publisher.

All the Internet addresses (URLs) given in this book were valid at the time of going to press. However, due to the dynamic nature of the Internet, some addresses may have changed, or sites may have changed or ceased to exist since publication. While the author and publisher regret any inconvenience this may cause readers, no responsibility for any such changes can be accepted by either the author or the publisher.

Contents

What did the Vikings do for me? 4

Who were the Vikings? 6

What was Viking society like? 8

How did the Vikings build ships? 12

Who were the Viking raiders? 14

What new worlds did the
    Vikings explore? 20

Where are the Vikings today? 26

Key dates 28

Glossary 30

Find out more 31

Index 32

Look for the Then and Now boxes. They highlight parts of Viking culture that are present in our modern world.

Any words appearing in the text in bold, **like this**, are explained in the glossary.

What did the Vikings do for me?

The Vikings sailed in big, wooden ships across the North Sea and northern Atlantic Ocean, in search of gold, silver, and other treasures. Wherever they landed, they attacked towns and villages. Sometimes they burned houses, churches, and **monasteries**. Vikings were fierce warriors who were feared everywhere they went.

However, violent attacks and raids were not all there was to Viking society. The men spent most of their time working as farmers. They also fished, hunted, and built boats. The women cared for their children and households. When the men went to sea, the women ran the farms. Both men and women wore jewellery and wove cloth with beautiful designs.

Look at the Viking scene below. It seems very different to modern times, but you might be surprised to discover some things the Vikings did that we still do today.

Who were the Vikings?

About 14,000 years ago, settlers travelled west to what is now Norway and Sweden. Over time, they moved further west and south to Denmark. Today, we call these countries Scandinavia and the people Scandinavians.

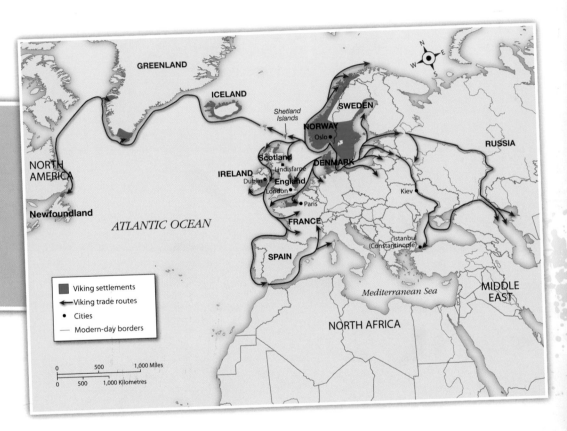

This map shows the main Viking settlements and trade routes during the **Viking Age** (AD 800–1100).

Viking settlements
Viking trade routes
Cities
Modern-day borders

Ancient Scandinavians

The early Scandinavians didn't settle in one place. Instead, they followed reindeer and other herds so that they could hunt them. This changed in about 4000 BC, when they began to settle down and farm the land. They had a short growing season during which they grew grains and vegetables. Cattle, sheep, goats, and pigs gave them meat and milk during the long, cold winters. They began to make metal tools, pottery, cloth, and jewellery.

All over Scandinavia, people had similar customs and beliefs. However, they began to think of themselves as different people. Some were Danes, some Norwegians, and some were Swedes. By about AD 500, these groups traded with other Europeans.

Religion

Christianity came to Europe by AD 100 or 200, but the Vikings kept their **pagan** beliefs for a long time. They worshipped many gods, including Odin, the god of war, and Thor, the god of thunder. Pleasing the gods was important to the Vikings. Warriors believed that if they died bravely in battle, they would live forever with Odin, in his palace, Valhalla.

This painting from 1872 shows the Viking god Thor fighting giants.

Wednesday, Thursday, Friday

Three days of the week are named after Viking gods. Wednesday comes from Odin, the god of war, who was also sometimes called Woden. Thursday is named after Thor, the god of thunder. Freya, the goddess of love, gave her name to Friday.

What was Viking society like?

Most Vikings were farmers. A farmer's household was made up of grandparents, parents, children, aunts, uncles, cousins, servants, and slaves.

Farms

Whole farming families lived together in a longhouse. This was a house made up of one large room, about 12–15 metres (40–50 feet) long. Sometimes one bedroom was screened off, but usually all family members slept together in one room. There was a fireplace in the middle, for warmth and cooking. Many farmers also had barns. Some farmers even had a dairy and a blacksmith's **forge**.

This modern reconstruction shows what a Viking longhouse would have looked like.

THEN...

The Vikings invented ice skates. They used horse or cow bones strapped to their feet with leather. They pushed themselves across the ice with a long stick. Bone skates were slow. Skaters could only go about 4 kilometres (2.5 miles) an hour.

Transport

Farms were often by the coast, or near rivers and lakes. During the warm months, the Vikings used boats to travel from farm to farm. When the water froze over in winter, they needed skates, skis, and sledges instead. The sledges were pulled by horses. The Vikings would fasten iron **cleats**, called frost-nails, to the horses' hooves. This meant that the horses would not slip and slide all over the ice!

Skis

Early paintings show that Viking hunters used skis to go hunting in winter. The skis were not so different from today. They were made from two curved planks with leather straps to slide the feet into.

This illustration from the 1500s shows Viking hunters using skis.

...NOW

Skates have changed a lot! Between **AD** 1200 and 1400, iron began to be used instead of bone. By the 1700s, steel blades were fitted to leather boots. Today, blades are so thin and light that a good skater can go as fast as 24 kilometres (15 miles) an hour.

Kingdoms

By the beginning of the **Viking Age** (about AD 800 to 1100), dozens of small kingdoms or chiefdoms existed throughout Scandinavia. A king would promise to protect the people from attack. In return, the people promised to be loyal to the king.

Vikings in Iceland held a yearly meeting, or *thing*, at Thingvellir, near the coast.

THEN...

Viking criminal trials took place at the *thing*. A group of 12 men, called a **jury**, would decide whether the accused was guilty or innocent. Occasionally the guilty were outlawed and could be killed, but usually they would only have to repay their victim.

Things

Each kingdom held a meeting once or twice a year called a *thing*. Nearly all men, except slaves, went to the meeting and many spoke there. If they were not pleased with their king, they chose a new one. They also made laws and settled arguments. Years later, the Vikings took the idea of the *thing* with them when they settled down in new lands.

Modern juries include both men and women. They include people from different backgrounds.

...NOW

The idea of trial by jury has spread to many countries around the world. Jury trials are common in the United Kingdom and the United States. However, in the United States, an accused person in a criminal trial can now decide to be tried by a judge rather than a jury.

How did the Vikings build ships?

In the AD 700s, Scandinavia had few cities or towns. Most people lived along the coasts on large farms. They used boats for fishing and trading with one another. People from Europe visited the coastal farms, looking for furs, timber, and other goods. Sea-trade with Europe grew.

Viking warships were called longships. They were fast and sturdy, and could hold 60 men. The longships were carried along on the wind by sails. On days when there was little wind, the men rowed the boats through the water. Both ends of a longship were the same shape. This meant that a ship could change direction on a narrow river without having to turn around.

Viking sails were made from wool, which has a natural oil in it called lanolin. This oil made the sails waterproof.

THEN...

Viking shipbuilders used iron **rivets** (metal pins) to fasten overlapping planks, or boards, together. These **clinker-built** ships were fast, and they worked equally well in shallow or deep waters. Most boats need time to swell when they are first put in the water, or they will leak. Not the clinker-built boats. They can be sailed as soon as they hit the water.

Ships used for trading were called knarrs. They were shorter and broader than a longship, and had plenty of space to carry goods to trade. The Vikings also used knarrs to move all their belongings and animals when they settled in a new country.

Notice how the boards overlap on this modern clinker-built fishing boat.

...NOW

Wooden boat builders throughout the world continue to make clinker-built boats. Overlapping wooden boards make for fast and sturdy fishing boats, rowboats, and yachts. These boats use oars, sails, and even motors to glide through the water. Several boat-building schools throughout the world teach students to build boats like the Vikings did.

Who were the Viking raiders?

In AD 793, some Vikings attacked a **monastery** at Lindisfarne, an island off the north-east coast of England. They arrived in small boats, rushed ashore, and stole gold, silver, and other valuable items. They were so fierce, strong, and unbeatable that they spread fear all over Britain. This raid marks the beginning of the **Viking Age**.

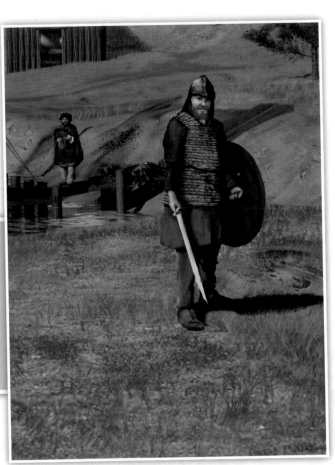

Viking raiders were armed with swords, spears, and axes. They carried shields for protection. Wealthy leaders also wore iron helmets and chain mail tunics.

THEN...

While they were away, farmers depended on their wives to run the farms. They held a ceremony handing the keys to their wives. If a Viking died at sea, his wife became owner of the farm and could sell it or keep it running. If a Viking woman divorced her husband, she kept part of the household wealth. Viking law gave women property rights.

Some of these frightening fighters were full-time warriors, but many were just farmers. They left on raids in the spring, after all their crops were planted. They came home in midsummer for the harvest. Then they would set off on another raid in the autumn.

While the Viking men left on raids, the women looked after the houses and farms.

...NOW

The Vikings were ahead of the rest of the world in recognizing women's rights and abilities. Unfortunately, many of those rights were lost over time. It was not until the 1800s that laws were passed in the United Kindom, the United States, and much of Europe that gave women the right to own and control property. Today, women in most countries around the world can own their own property. However, there are still many places where women are not treated equally to men.

Moving in

Viking kings grew rich from their raids. They were able to train and equip large armies. In AD 841, one of these armies landed in Ireland. They conquered Ulster and founded a settlement that would become Dublin. Instead of raiding and then returning home as they had once done, the Vikings settled in Ireland. However, this didn't mean they stopped raiding! Using Ireland as a base, the Vikings attacked towns, **monasteries**, and farms in Scotland and England.

In AD 865, a Viking army from Denmark invaded England. The next year, this army captured the city of York and settled there. They called it Jorvik. They built houses with thatched roofs, farmed, and set up businesses. As the population grew, they added new streets and buildings.

Craftsmen made combs, knives, jewellery, shoe buckles, leather goods, and pottery. Traders took these goods all over Europe. When they came home, the traders brought clothing, spices, and perfumes. Jorvik became a famous trading centre.

Combs

Viking combs could be made from wood or bones, or deer, reindeer, and elk antlers. They could be single- or double-sided. The wealthy owned combs with delicate carvings on them, while the poor had very simple ones.

THEN...

Both English and the Viking language, called Old Norse, are Germanic languages. This means that the English and the Vikings were probably able to understand each other. Over time, the languages began to blend even more, and many Old Norse words became part of English.

These Viking combs and hair picks were found in Ireland.

...NOW

We still use many Viking words today. For example, *egg*, *root*, and *kid* came from Old Norse. Also, *sister* and *husband*, as well as *anger*, *cake*, *fellow*, *get*, *rug*, *scrub*, *skin*, *take*, and *ugly*. There are many others, including a lot of words to do with the law, farming, and trade.

Normans

At the same time as some Viking armies were attacking Britain, others were invading France. In AD 885, an army of 30,000 Vikings marched on Paris. They held it for two months, but were defeated. Instead, they settled down to farm in Normandy, in northern France. They became known as Normans, and began to speak French and to take on French customs.

During the Viking battle at Suffolk in AD 869, Vikings attacked and murdered the British King Edmund.

Berserkers

Berserkers were fierce Viking warriors who howled and bit their shields before battle. They believed that their anger gave them strength.

THEN...

Fear of Viking raids forced people throughout Europe to unite into nations. According to experts, this was a major change in the history of Europe. Small kingdoms had a difficult time defending themselves, but when they joined together they became stronger. In England, the rule of William the Conqueror halted further Viking attacks.

The Danelaw

By AD 885, all of north-east England was under Viking control. This area became known as the Danelaw, and stretched from north of York all the way to London in the south. The Danelaw followed Viking laws and customs.

Later on, a new wave of Vikings attacked and conquered England. The leaders of these new groups became kings of England. However, in 1066, the Norman duke William the Conqueror invaded Britain from across the English Channel. William became the new ruler of England.

On this map, the purple line divides England. All of the land to the north-east was called the Danelaw, and was under Viking rule.

...NOW

Although history doesn't tell us if this was a direct result of the Vikings, this pattern of large, powerful nations continues today. The countries in Britain joined to become the United Kingdom. Even in America, the colonies found strength in joining together to form one nation, the United States. Larger nations are better able to defend themselves and to grow strong.

What new worlds did the Vikings explore?

The Vikings were forced to look for new lands to settle because they were running out of good farmland at home. They were helped in this by changes in the climate. The weather became warmer than it had been in earlier centuries. This meant that the Vikings could explore new lands for a longer part of the year.

Iceland

By AD 870, the Vikings had moved further west to Iceland. Even though farming was difficult in the cold, windy island, the settlements there grew rapidly. By AD 930, there were 30,000 people. A hundred years later, this figure had doubled to 60,000.

In Iceland, the Vikings established a **thing** to make and enforce laws. It became known as the *Althing*, and it still survives today as Iceland's national parliament.

Furs for nuts

Greenland's Viking settlers traded polar bear skins, walrus ivory, and furs for timber, tools, and special treats like raisins and nuts.

THEN...

Some experts call the Vikings the first oceanographers. Viking settlers used ocean currents to decide where to build towns and farms. In AD 874, Ingólfur Arnarson threw wooden pillars overboard as he approached Iceland. He made his home where the wood landed (present-day Reykjavik, Iceland's capital). He knew that the ocean currents that guided the wood to land would also help ships find their way.

Greenland

In AD 982, the Viking Eric the Red set sail westwards from Iceland. He saw a new land covered with ice. He called his discovery Greenland. It was colder than Iceland and it wasn't green, but he hoped that naming it Greenland would encourage others to join his settlement. The first settlers built dairy and sheep farms. Under Eric's leadership, Greenland's population reached 3,000.

This modern painting shows Eric the Red setting sail for Greenland with the crew of his Viking longship.

...NOW

Today, ships still use ocean currents to cut fuel costs. For example, a major shipping company in Japan tracks ocean currents. Then it guides its fleet of large oil carriers into the currents to save fuel.

America

When Leif Eriksson, son of Erik the Red, heard rumours of an unexplored land to the west, he set off to find it. He reached Labrador, in Canada sometime between AD 997 and 1003. He called it *Markland*, or Forest Land, and settled there for the winter.

Viking sagas tell of four other journeys to America between AD 1000 and 1030. Vikings settled at L'Anse aux Meadows in Newfoundland, Canada. They used it as a base while exploring the North Atlantic coast. The land was excellent for farming and timber, but the small band of Vikings could not defend themselves against the large numbers of Native Americans who already lived there. They returned to Iceland.

The Vikings called the Native Americans *skraelings*, which may have meant "screamers" or "screaming weaklings". However, the Native Americans were actually strong and frightening. One of the first meetings between the Vikings and *skraelings* ended in a deadly battle. The Vikings killed eight Native Americans. The *skraelings* fought back and killed the Viking leader.

The first Norwegian-American

Snorri Thorfinnsson, who was born between AD 1004 and 1013 in L'Anse aux Meadows, is thought to be the first European born in North America. When he was a child, his family returned to Iceland. Snorri Thorfinnsson became an important Icelandic leader.

THEN...

Wherever the Vikings went, they settled down. Warriors would marry local women and have families. Their children often looked like them, so Viking features were passed on to their **descendants**.

Several Viking accounts tell of battles between Viking warriors and Native Americans.

...NOW

Many people in the United Kingdom are descended from Vikings. It is thought that up to 50 per cent of people in some parts of north-east England might have a Viking **ancestor**. There area probably the same number of Viking descendants in Ireland and Scotland, too.

Russia and the East

While Vikings from Denmark and Norway headed west and south, the Swedes travelled east. Most Swedish Vikings were settlers and traders, not pirates. In AD 858, they captured present-day Kiev and Novgorod. From here, they spread into neighbouring villages. These Swedish settlers were called the Rus.

At first the Rus were outsiders, but soon they began marrying people from the area, speaking their language, and even taking their names.

Traders

Some Swedish Vikings set up farms in Russia. Others began trading. Viking traders travelled 800 kilometres (500 miles) along the River Dnieper to the Black Sea. They crossed

Russia
The country Russia gets its name from the Rus, the Vikings who invaded it so long ago.

the sea to Constantinople, which is now known as Istanbul and is the capital of Turkey. The markets in Constantinople had riches from all over Asia, such as spices, silks, and jewellery. The Vikings took their own goods there to sell.

THEN...

Viking trade routes stretched from Greenland in the west to Turkey in the east. Traders carried goods and information all along their routes. They showed people things they had never dreamed of before. For example, a small, bronze Buddha statue from India has been found in far away Sweden!

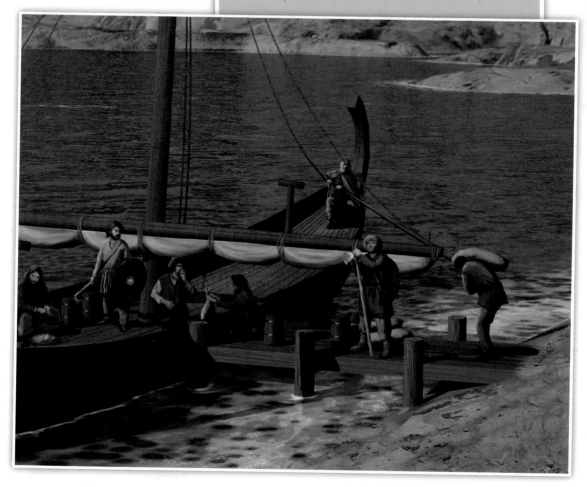

Here, Viking goods are being loaded on to a trading ship, known as a knarr. They will be transported to distant lands for trading.

...NOW

Today we depend on worldwide trade. Goods made in China are sold all over the world. Japanese cars can be bought in Europe. African coffee is used everywhere. Trade is greater and faster today than it was in the **Viking Age**, but we like foreign goods just as much as the Vikings did! Even though the Vikings probably did not invent the concept of global trade, they no doubt had a huge influence on it throughout history.

Where are the Vikings today?

The Vikings are not forgotten today. We use Old Norse words every day and live in cities first built by the Vikings. We may know people who are the **descendants** of Vikings, or be descended from them ourselves.

Celebrating the Vikings

Viking stories still capture our imaginations. Children and adults enjoy dressing up as Vikings. **Re-enactment** societies all over the world hold pretend battles. People wear Viking clothing and carry axes and swords. No one gets hurt. It's just for fun!

This photograph shows the celebration of Up Helly Aa, a Scottish fire festival. People burn Viking-style ships, dress as Vikings, and sing songs in Old Norse.

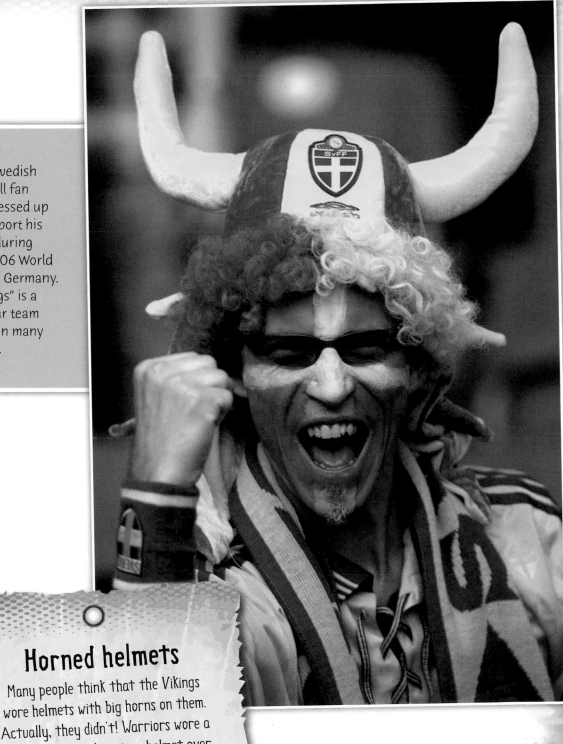

This Swedish football fan has dressed up to support his team during the 2006 World Cup in Germany. "Vikings" is a popular team name in many sports.

Horned helmets

Many people think that the Vikings wore helmets with big horns on them. Actually, they didn't! Warriors wore a sheepskin cap with an iron helmet over it. A metal piece came down in front to cover the warrior's nose.

Key dates

Here is an outline of important moments in the history and culture of the Vikings:

14,000 years ago	Settlers move into Scandinavia from the east
4,000 years ago	Ancient Scandinavians begin farming
AD 500	Scandinavians are trading with other Europeans
700	The Vikings excel at shipbuilding
793	A raid on Lindisfarne marks the beginning of the **Viking Age**
832	Ireland is raided three times in one month
841	Vikings conquer Ulster and found a settlement that will become Dublin
858	Swedish Vikings take over Novgorod and Kiev

866	A Viking army captures York and some Vikings begin settling down in the lands they have invaded
870–930	Vikings settle in Iceland
885–86	Vikings attack Paris
900	Vikings settle in north-west England
907	Vikings reach Constantinople and begin trading with the city
911	Vikings settle in Normandy
940–954	The Vikings and the English fight over York
986	Eric the Red leads the settlement of Greenland
Late 900s	Voyages to North America begin
990–1030	Vikings settle in present-day Canada
1066	The Battle of Hastings marks the end of the Viking era

Glossary

AD short for Anno Domini, which is Latin for "in the year of our Lord". AD is used for all the years after year 1.

ancestors all the past members of a family. Many people today have Viking ancestors.

BC short for before Christ. BC is used for all the years before year 1.

cleat metal strips designed to protect against slipping. Boots with cleats help us walk on ice.

clinker-built ship built with overlapping boards. Viking boats were clinker-built.

descendant someone's descendants are the people who live at a future date in the same family. The Vikings left descendants wherever they settled.

forge blacksmith's workshop. Viking farms often had a forge.

jury group of people chosen to make a decision. Viking juries judged criminals and solved problems.

monastery place where monks live and worship. Vikings raided monasteries looking for gold.

pagan person who believes in more than one god. Vikings were pagans.

re-enactment perform something again. Re-enactment societies perform Viking battles in modern times.

rivet metal pin used to hold pieces together. Viking boat builders used rivets to hold the wood together.

thing assembly held once or twice a year in Viking settlements. Viking laws were made at *things*.

Viking Age period between AD 800 to 1100, when the Vikings raided, explored, and traded all over the world. The Viking Age was a time of great change.

Find out more

Books

History From Objects: The Vikings, John Malam (Wayland, 2010)

The Gruesome Truth About: The Vikings, Matt Buckingham (Wayland, 2010)

Tracking Down: The Vikings in Britain, Moira Butterfield (Franklin Watts, 2010)

Websites

www.bbc.co.uk/schools/primaryhistory/vikings/
This website has lots of information about Viking culture in Britain.

www.mnh.si.edu/vikings/start.html
Find out more about the Viking exploration of Greenland and North America on this useful website.

www.pbs.org/wgbh/nova/vikings/
This web page has lots of information on Viking history. You can explore a Viking village and learn how to write your name in the Viking alphabet.

A place to visit

JORVIK Viking Centre
Coppergate
York YO1 9WT
www.jorvik-viking-centre.co.uk

Index

Althing 20
America 19, 22–23
armies 16
Arnarson, Ingólfur 20

berserkers 18

Canada 22
Christianity 7
cleats 9
clinker-built boats
    12, 13
combs 16, 17
Constantinople 24
craftsmen 16
criminal trials 10, 11

Danelaw 19
days of the week 7
Denmark 6, 16
descendants 22,
    23, 26
divorce 14

Edmund, King 18
Erik the Red 21, 22
Eriksson, Leif 22

farming 6, 8, 14, 15,
    17, 20, 21, 24
fire festivals 26
France 18

gods and goddesses 7
Greenland 21, 24

helmets 27
horses 9
hunting 6, 9

ice skates 8, 9
Iceland 10, 20
Ireland 16

jewellery 5, 6, 16
Jorvik 16
juries 10, 11

Kiev 24
kingdoms 10–11, 18
knarrs 13

Labrador 22
languages 16, 17
laws 11, 15, 17, 19, 20
Lindisfarne 14
longhouses 8
longships 12

monasteries 14

Native Americans
    22, 23
Newfoundland 22
Normans 18
Norway 6
Novgorod 24

ocean currents 20, 21
oceanographers 20
Old Norse language
    16, 17, 26

pagans 7
property rights 14, 15

raids 4, 14–15, 16,
    18, 19

re-enactment
    societies 26
religion 7
rivets 12
Rus 24
Russia 24

sagas 22
Scandinavians 6–7
settlements 16, 20,
    21, 22
ships and boats 9,
    12–13
skis 9
slaves 11
sledges 9
society 8–11
Sweden 6
Swedish Vikings 24

thing 10, 11, 20
Thorfinnsson, Snorri 22
trade 7, 12, 13, 16,
    17, 20, 24, 25
transport 9

United Kingdom 19
United States 19
Up Helly Aa 26

Valhalla 7
Viking Age 10, 14

William the
    Conqueror 18, 19
women 5, 14, 15

York 16, 19